Social

The Art of Marketing YouTube, Facebook, Twitter, and Instagram for Success

By Calvin Kennedy

Table of Contents

Introduction

Some entrepreneurs see social media marketing as the next big thing, a powerful but temporary fad that has to be taken advantage of it while it's in the spotlight. To others, it's just a buzzword that doesn't have a practical advantage, and there's a complicated, steep learning curve with it.

Due to the rapid pace in which social media has developed its reputation, some business owners perceive this as a passing marketing interest, therefore, it is presumed non-profitable. However, the statistics are illustrating different results. Hubspot reported that 92% of marketers in 2014 claimed social media marketing was imperative for their business, with 80% indicating social media marketing efforts have increased traffic to their websites. 97% of marketers, according to Social Media Examiner, participate in social media marketing, but 85% of participants are not sure what social media marketing tools are the best ones to use, as well as how they should be marketing on social media, to begin with.

This demonstrates that social media marketing has a huge potential for an increase in sales, but there's a lack of understanding amongst entrepreneurs on how to achieve those results. Before we get into how you can insert yourself into the social media marketing arena successfully, let's look at how social media marketing can benefit you and your business.

Increases Brand Recognition

Each opportunity a business owner has to syndicate their content and increase their visibility to their potential clients and customers, as well as their current ones, is of great value. Social media networks are just a new channel for your company to voice their opinion and boost their product and service's exposure. This is imperative for your business because it makes your business more accessible to new clients and customers, it also makes you more recognized and familiar for those who have already done business with you. For example, frequent Twitter users might hear about your company for the first time only after they've stumbled on it in their newsfeed. Perhaps a customer who is otherwise apathetic might become more acquainted with your business and brand after they've seen your presence on many different networks.

Improves Brand Loyalty

Brands that engage with their social media channels have a higher loyalty rate with their customers. Companies ought to take advantage of the tools that social media has given them when it comes to connecting with an audience. An open and strategic social media plan proves influential when it comes to making people loyal to a brand.

More Opportunities to Convert

Every post you put on social media networks is an opportunity for a customer or client to convert. When you build followings, you're simultaneously gaining access to new customers, old customers, and recent customers. You can even interact with all of them at the same time. Every image, blog post, video, or comment you decide to share is a chance for someone to react to what you've posted, and every reaction can lead to site visits, and eventually, conversions. Not every contact with your business on social media is going to result in a conversion, but every positive contact will increase the likelihood of a potential conversion. Even if your click-through rate is low, the sheer amount of opportunities you have is a game changer.

Higher Conversion Rates

Social media marketing will result in a higher conversion rate in a few different ways. The most significant way is the humanization element. Your brand is becoming more humanized when you interact on social media platforms. Social media is a place where brands are able to act like people do, and this is imperative because people like to do business with other people, not with a company.

In addition, studies demonstrate that social media has a one hundred percent higher initial contact to close rate than outbound marketing, and a greater amount of followers on social media tends to improve credibility and trust in your brand. Due to this, just building your audience on social media platforms improves your conversion rates on your existing traffic.

In addition, your brand will seem more authoritative to new users. If you interact with major influencers on Twitter or other social media platforms, your visible authority reach is going to increase greatly.

People like to interact with businesses that they see as being the best in their specific industry or niche.

Increased Inbound Traffic

If you don't have a social media account, your inbound traffic is going to be limited to the people who are already familiar with your company and individuals who are searching for keywords you're ranked for on search engines. Each social media profile you have is another path that leads back to your site, and every post, like, comment, or share you make is another opportunity for a new visitor to interact with you. The more quality content you have on social media platforms, the more inbound traffic you're going to obtain, and more traffic mean more leads, which eventually leads to more conversions.

Decreased Marketing Costs

According to a study conducted by Hubspot, 84% of businesses discovered that just six hours of effort a week was enough to create an increased amount of traffic to their sites. Six hours is not a huge investment for channels as large as social media platforms. If you can lend just an hour a day to developing content and posting strategies, you will begin to see the results of your efforts almost immediately. Even paid advertising through Twitter and Facebook is pretty cheap, depending on your goals. Begin small, and you won't ever have to worry about going over your budget. Once you have a better feel for what you can expect on these platforms, you can increase the budget and increase the conversions you have at the same time.

Search Engine Rankings Increase

SEO is the greatest way to capture relevant traffic from the search engines, but the necessities for being on the top are always fluctuating. It's no longer enough that you update your blog on a regular basis, ensure that optimized title tags and Meta descriptions have been filled in and that distribution links are pointing back to your site. Search engines such as Google and Bing might be calculating their ranking using social media presence as a big aspect because of the fact that solid brands tend to use social media.

Consequently, being visible on social media might act as a brand signal to a search engine that your brand is a legitimate, trustworthy, and credible one. This means that if you want to rank for a given keyword, having a strong presence on social media might be mandatory.

Better Customer Experiences

At its core, social media is a communication channel like phone calls and emails. Each customer interaction you have on social media is an opportunity to demonstrate to the public your customer service level, and it is an opportunity to make your relationship with your customers better. For example, if someone were to complain about a product on Facebook, you could address the complaint, apologize to them publicly, and take action to make the situation right. Or, if someone compliments you, you could thank and recommend some additional products for them. It's the personal experience that demonstrates to customers that you truly care about them.

Better Customer Awareness

Social media gives your company the opportunity to gain some valuable information about what potential customers are interested in and how they behave in a social setting. For example, you can watch comments to see what people think about your business directly or watch for comments that are directed toward your industry. You can split up your content into lists based on the topic and see what types of content get the most interest out of customers, and then produce more of that content type. You can measure the conversions you get based on the different promotions that are posted on different social media platforms and find the perfect combination that will generate revenue for your business.

There are numerous benefits to getting on social media if you're a business, but all those benefits come down to one thing – you get more exposure for your business, which translates to more sales. Your bottom line is going to thank you for investing a little bit of time and effort into your social media efforts.

Chapter One – The Social Media Marketing Plan, Why You Need One

Social media marketing plans are in-depth outlines of everything you want to achieve by making your company active on social media. Without a solid plan, social media marketing feels like a meaningless task, and your potential for success suffers greatly without direction.

While social media might have seemed like the Wild West of a brand's marketing efforts, the outlet for advertising has matured to the point where it provides companies with concrete, real, and measurable impacts on their business' profits. Social media marketing has to work in sync with the rest of the business strategy to ensure that the overall goals of the brand are being attained.

There are six steps to creating a social media marketing plan, which we're going to explore in the remainder of this chapter. Remember, a social media plan is just like any other area of your business plan, which means it requires details in order to be impactful on your business.

Step One: Make Goals for Your Social Media Impact

Just like any other marketing plan, the first step to a solid one is to set goals. Outlining your goals provides you with a clear way to measure the success of your marketing plan, and it is a way you can keep track of the return on investment (ROI). Social media marketing helps your business reach numerous goals, but some of the most common ones you might want to include are:

- Brand awareness increases
- Improving customer loyalty and increasing sales
- Increasing customer and potential customer engagement with the company
- Increasing traffic to a website
- Improving the customer service division
- Increasing the number of followers or fans, which will increase the amount of potential customers

While all of these goals are a great way to begin, it's important that you begin by focusing on just one or two of them at a time. Creating goals for a social media marketing plan is just like anything else in life – you do not want to start out too broad with a goal, as this would mean that you've spread your resources too thin and you risk not achieving your main purpose.

One of the best ways to set up a goal, whether it's personal or business-related, is to create a SMART goal. If you've read about these before, it's because SMART goals are just that intelligent, and they work. If you're not familiar with the acronym SMART, it means, Specific, Measurable, Achievable, Realistic, and Timely.

Let's take a look at each letter in more depth, in case you're not familiar with this form of goal setting or you need a refresher.

Specific

There isn't any point in being vague about the goals you're setting. Otherwise, you won't have a clear target you can aim for. Therefore, be specific. For example:

Increase the website traffic to our company blog using links shared twice a week on social media profiles such as Facebook and Twitter.

Measurable

If you want to know whether your social media marketing plan and subsequent actions are making your company money or increasing exposure to potential customers or clients, then you need to make measurable goals. Vague, immeasurable goals might allow you to see a slight improvement or guess at one, but a measurable goal is more specific than that. It could be something such as:

Increase the website traffic to our company blog referred by social media channels by 20%.

Attainable

This is the number one mistake many companies and individuals make when they're setting a goal. They make it unattainable because they want to accomplish everything at once. There isn't an easy button for goals. If you try to push too far, you'll set yourself up for failure right away. Therefore, make your goals challenging, but also make sure they're realistic. For example:

Increase the website traffic to our company blog with social media channels by 20% from 1,000 unique visitors to 1,200 unique visitors.

Relevant

Make sure that your social media goals are actually in line with the rest of your business goal; otherwise, you'll quickly become frustrated. For example:

Gaining traffic to your blog is going to expose audiences to your free product guides and industry insights, and encourage them to obtain a subscription to your mailing list for further information and updates that will, in turn, encourage them to purchase products and services from your company.

Timely

Lastly, you need to set a timeframe for the goal. Without a timeframe, goals are open-ended and don't encourage you to set up small goals along the way to meet a deadline. Timeframes help you stay accountable, driven, and less likely to stray from the path when it comes to putting a plan in action. For example:

We want to increase our website traffic to our blog using social media outlets by the end of the fourth quarter in 2017.

Step Two: Create Social Media Profiles (Or Spruce up Old Ones)

You have your goals pinned down, so it's time to start creating profiles that will wow your potential customers and clients.

There are a few mini steps to this one. So let's begin with the first one – figuring out what social media networks you should join.

What Social Networks to Join

There are unique aspects to every social media outlet out there. What works on one social media network isn't going to work on another, and the primary characteristics of each network can vary greatly. You don't need to be active on every social media network! The key is to focus on just one or two that will help you best achieve your social media marketing plan.

The audiences and demographics of social networks are arguably the most imperative factor you need to consider. You've most likely already obtained a good idea of where your customers tend to hang out online, but reports such as *The Demographics of Social Media Users* by Pew Research Center lay out some concrete data for the five largest social networks – Pinterest, Facebook, Twitter, Instagram, and LinkedIn.

Other factors to consider are how much time you have to dedicate to advertising on social media and what resources are available to you. These will help you figure out which social network is the best fit for your company.

Optimizing the Social Media Profiles

An up-to-date, complete social media profile will give your visitors a good first impression. It will highlight your company's professionalism, and show people you're ready for business. It's a good idea to refresh profiles from time to time, but it's crucial you start off on the right foot.

- Upload the profile photos and cover photos that have been optimized for your social media profile.
- Complete the About and Bio sections for each network fully, tailoring the text to the audience of the social media network you've joined.

Perform an Audit for Yourself and Competitors

If you've already created a presence on social media sites, the time you plan out a marketing plan is the perfect time to perform an audit. Audits ensure all your social media profiles are up to date, and it gives you an insight into how competitors are performing. Take a look at the following checklists to help you get started with an in-depth audit of your profiles and your competitor's profiles.

Your Company's Profile

1. Find and take note of every social media profile your company has, unofficial and official. Profiles and fan pages set up by employees or followers should be merged or purged to avoid confusion.

2. Make sure your profile and cover photos are all up to date and consistent with your company's branding.

3. Update the Bios and About sections with current information and messaging, using the tone and language that is best suited to the social network you're using. For example, Facebook is more laid back than LinkedIn.

4. Take note of the follower and fan accounts of the profiles, and when the last activity was recorded. If one account is starting to lag behind the others, even if you're still posting, consider whether it's worth your time to carry on with that platform or whether your efforts would be best focused somewhere else.

Competitor Profiles

1. Find a few social media accounts run by your company's competitors, either from one network or a variety of networks.
2. Take note of how often those companies' pages are updated with new posts, what they're posting, and what type of engagement the posts receive on average in the forms of shares, likes, and comments.
3. Write down the date and their current number of followers and likes on their profile, which is a benchmark for you to work out their growth versus your company's growth at a later time.
4. Examine the branding of their profile – profile photo, cover photo, and their tone. Do they give a good reflection of the brand's

offering, the brand, and the brand's personality? Is it something you'd like to emulate, or do you want to stay away from it?

Step Three: Establishing a Tone of Voice

Just as with any form of marketing, the way you speak or write to your audience has a significant impact on how they view your company and you. Brand personality is a set of associative and emotional characteristics that are connected to a brand or company name. These things will shape how people view a company and how they interact with a company. Often, brand's personalities mirror that of their target customers.

You might already have a decent idea of what your brand's personality is like, but the following set of questions will make sure everyone on your team has a consistent point of reference to use.

- If your company or brand was a person, what type of personality would it have?
- If your brand was a person, what would their relationship be with the consumer? Would they be like a friend, a coach, a teacher, a parental figure, etc.?

- Write down what your company's personality is not, using adjectives.

- Are there companies that have similar personalities to your brand? Why are these companies similar?

- How do you want customers to view your company or brand?

Once you've answered these questions, you ought to have a good idea about the tone your social media marketing is going to have, and you'll be setup to start creating and publishing content, but let's look at step four before you get into that.

Step Four: Creating a Post Strategy

You can have the best looking social media profile and the best intentions in the world, but when you don't have a content plan and a posting strategy, all those efforts can go to waste. Rather than plowing ahead without a plan, take a little time to build a posting strategy that is going to knock the competition right out of the water. Consider the following points:

- What forms of content are you going to post, and who is going to be responsible for creating that content? Images are a necessity with most social media platforms, but video content is becoming a central medium to many companies' content strategies. Other forms of content include statistics, quotes, quizzes, comics, and so much more.

- How often are you going to post, and at what times during the day? There's always a debate going on about what posting frequency and times of the day are the best to post. The truth is, there isn't a one size fits all solution to this. The answer to that question is unique to your company and audience. How often you want to post is going to depend on the industry you're in, your capability to make and curate good content, your reach, and the social network you're using. As a general rule, businesses ought to aim to post on Facebook one or two times a day, five times or more per day on Twitter, and once a day on LinkedIn and Instagram. What time of day you post content should be determined by past history, or by targeting your fans when they're most likely to be active on social media, such as before work in the morning, after work in the evening, or anytime during the weekends.

- How are you going to promote content using both free and paid strategies? Without a loyal, large, and engaged audience, posting an update and hoping for it to do well isn't going to work for you in the long term. With competition from attention in the social media feeds of your fans, posting the same content many times in different guises, as well as targeting them using paid promotions, should be a big part of your strategy.

An excellent way to keep track of your progress and when to post is to keep a social media content calendar. This will help you plan for weeks or months ahead of time and give you an idea of the content you'll be posting on social media. This will help prevent you from posting inconsistently and randomly, and it will let you build themes into your updates weekly, monthly, and seasonally.

Spontaneous posting on social media still does have its place, such as in response to breaking news or a customer service crisis that has to be addressed immediately, but for the main part of your marketing strategy, a content calendar is a good step.

Step Five: Experiment and Analyze

There isn't a magic bullet when it comes to social media marketing success. The most posts are put out by your company, and the more you experiment, the more you'll find out what content is going to work best for your company, what times of the day are best for engagement activity, and how often you need to post new stuff. Most importantly, your social marketing plan ought to never be static. You should do more things that work, but always be open to experimenting with new content, especially if it's new in the industry new for your company.

Instead of guessing, the easiest way to know what's working and what's not is to use a reporting tool. Sites such as Twitter, Facebook, and Pinterest have built-in analytics you can use that give you a good idea of the performance of your profile and growth, such as post and page likes, popular posts, audience demographics, and a lot more. However, you might want to consider a central reporting tool, such as Hootsuite, to keep it all in one place.

Other ways you can measure the success of your social media marketing plan is to include link shorteners that keep track of the clicks on the link, and the social section of the Google analytics is a good tool for observing the impact of social media marketing on your website.

Structured Testing Method

There are times when the amount of figures and charts become overwhelming, so here's one way you can structure your social media experiments clearly.

1. Choose what it is you want to test. Is it the engagement rate on your video posts? The website referrals you get? The reach of your images? Pick just one.

2. Set a goal. After a certain period, a week or a month, check the statistics on the factor you've chosen to test and take note of it. This is going to be your benchmark for the following segment of testing.

3. Double-down or try something new. Experiment with variations of your posting strategy, and then revisit that goal after another period of time to see whether performance has declined, improved, or

stayed the same. Depending on the results, alter the strategy to optimize it and make it a regular part of the marketing plan. If it doesn't work, then try something new again.

4. Did you meet the goal?

Step Six: Automate the Process, Engage with Followers, and Listen

The most wonderful thing about a detail social media marketing plan is you get to prepare the bulk of your content strategies ahead of time, and then you can use automation tools to queue your content, publish it, and distribute it exactly as your marketing plan schedule has dictated. Hootsuite, Post Planner, and Buffer are all great tools to check out.

When your posting schedule has been automated, you free up your time to engage with your audience. You can set aside time on a daily basis to chat and interact with customers who are engaging with your content, answer questions, and thank people who have shared your posts, as well as active searching and native notifications, tools such as Mention and Google Alerts send you emails when someone has mentioned your brand online, which prompts you to re-share or interact with that post.

When you have a social media marketing plan in place, you feel a lot more confident about using social media to market your business. You're much better prepared to reach your goals for social media marketing. Remember these steps, create your plan, and you'll be well on your way to social media marketing success!

Chapter Two – Marketing to Clientele on Facebook

The number one most popular platform that numerous businesses choose to begin marketing on is Facebook and for a good reason. Facebook has over one billion active members on their site. That's a huge audience for your brand, but it means you have to be careful about where you spend your money advertising, and you have to have a very clear idea of the demographic for your brand. Knowing who will be interested in your product on Facebook could boost your sales phenomenally.

In this chapter, we're going to go over the most important features and tips for marketing on Facebook. You don't have to use all of these tips, but focusing on a few key tips and features can significantly boost your sales and your brand's reach.

Tips for Marketing on Facebook

As a business tool, Facebook is dominating the popularity contest as a key element of most marketing strategies for businesses. However, due to the longevity of Facebook posts, you might find you're struggling to come up with new content all the time and fresh ideas for your company or your brand's page.

While it's tempting to write up a bit of content, find some cute images, or post nonstop, approaching it with some strategy is going to improve your odds of engaging in valuable conversations with customers and your audience. The following tips are going to help you increase engagement on your marketing efforts.

Timing

While it depends on your target audience, content, and goals, the timing of your posts is something you need to consider seriously. Look at your targeted audience, note their personalities, and time your posts accordingly. For example, if you're targeting busy mothers who stay at home, the best time to reach them is most likely going to be different from reaching single bachelors.

One good way to figure out what times work best is through some trial and error, but there is another way to start out with a bit more accuracy. Studies have already been conducted to determine when different types of audiences are online, but a good beginning point is to start posting on Thursdays and Fridays because these are the most active days on Facebook. Engagement rates begin to drop by 3.5% below the average from Monday to Wednesday. In addition, one in the afternoon is the best time to post to get a share, and three is the best time to post to get a click.

However, these are not the most popular times to post on Facebook. It's the timing of your post that will show an increase in engagement and not the popular times for your audience to be posting.

Images

You've most likely heard this one a million times, but the benefits of adding images to the posts you put on

Facebook can't be emphasized enough. Photos will receive 84% more link clicks and 53% more likes on Facebook than the average post. Here are some useful tips for images on Facebook.

1. Share images of actual people
2. Use lifestyle imagery instead of product imagery
3. Focus on people's faces
4. Be concise
5. Create galleries
6. Encourage a short response
7. Use nostalgia to your advantage

Contests

People love getting free stuff. Everyone has found themselves liking and engaging with a branded Facebook page they wouldn't have been aware of if they have the opportunity to win something. The thrill of maybe getting something for free is one of the best incentives, and will most likely have very little cost to your business when compared to the awareness your brand will get from the contest.

The top reasons people 'like' brands on Facebook are so they can get a discount, promotion, or a giveaway.

While the idea of increasing engagement is good, there are seven real returns on investments that are seen with the usage of Facebook contests for brands.

1. It increases your fan base
2. It boosts your traffic
3. It produces user-generated content
4. It generates target market opinions
5. It increases virality and shares
6. It creates conversations
7. It grows your email list

Crowdsourced Answers

One of the benefits of hosting Facebook contests is a crowdsourcing customer and audience feedback to boost your Facebook engagement. Crowdsourcing is a kind of social listening, which is imperative to social media strategies. Everyone's favorite topic of conversation is themselves, so by turning to your Facebook fans to get opinions and ideas on something is an excellent way to increase engagement.

Ask a simple question of your current Facebook fans, or use a poll to get them to vote on a question, and you'll have an easy way to see exactly what your customers and audience want. Here are a few suggestions for crowdsourcing painlessly to get the most out of your audience.

1. Collect testimonials using questions
2. Gather your post comments
3. Ask your fans to send photos using the products they've purchased from your brand
4. Run a photo contest and collect images of your brand
5. Run a contest

Boost Posts

While there is some debate about this practice, boosting a company's Facebook post is still a good way to improve your reach and engagement potential with your audience. When you identify your target audience, you can hone in on those who you want to reach through boosting your posts. Boosted posts are posts that are paid for that appear higher up on an audience's news feed.

The fee will depend on how many people you'd like your post to reach, and the payment will depend on the number of impressions the post has over time. You don't want to boost every post you make on

Facebook, but things such as contests and highly active posts should be boosted. You'll want to look into boosting posts because:

1. It will help promote your products or services that are offered by your brand or business.
2. It will encourage visits to the company's website.
3. It will spread awareness to a limited-time campaign you're running.

Find Audience Insights

This tip goes together with crowdsourcing answers, and for a very good reason. The posts, activities, comments and other types of engagement you come across with your brand's Facebook page will offer you valuable information to consider. You will see what type of content your audience is going to respond to, what type of content they're going to ignore, and can determine what content you ought to concentrate on.

In addition, you'll be able to narrow in on what your audience is and focus on that demographic. Facebook makes this extremely easy for you with their Audience Insights page, where you're able to see what your audience engages with. You'll know if you need to post more text, photos, or videos, and what tone these posts should have.

Give Them Unique and Valuable Content

This might seem a little obvious, but the number of companies and brands who are relying on information that is obviously recycled or stale shows the degree of missed opportunities there is on Facebook. Hopefully, you've recognized who your target customer and audience is, so you need to carefully consider the content they're going to find most valuable. A teenage, suburban girl is most likely not going to care about the Four Ways to Store Tomatoes. Your common sense is going to help you with questions like this, so taking that extra second to stop and think about your audience is going to help you out a lot, and it will put you above your competition.

Remember, your product or your brand is unique. Whether you do or do not have direct competition doesn't matter, there are things that your product or service does that no one else is able to claim, so take advantage of them and highlight them through your Facebook page. Are there things customers can do that they couldn't do before thanks to your product?

Feature photos of them doing those things, or provide videos of your product or service helping someone.

If you're an expert in your field, offer them solutions and advice through your Facebook page. The possibilities are pretty much endless, so take the time to sit down and think about how your brand and products are different from your competition, and then highlight them in your posts.

Building Your Audience

While the previous section was about engaging with your current audience and perhaps a few new audience members, what about seriously building your audience in the beginning? Let's look at a few tips on how to accomplish this.

Email Acquisition with ActionSprout

Most people understand that the real battleground on Facebook is not the Facebook page, but the news feeds. In fact, very few users will actually visit the page; rather, they interact with the page updates that are in their news feeds.

The problem with most page apps for Facebook is that they require a user to visit the page. For example, a photo contest will require that the user visits a custom tab on the Facebook page of the company to upload their photo and submit their contest entry. Therefore, they have to leave their news feed, which is their home away from home, in order to participate in the contest.

ActionSprout will remove this barrier by allowing you to put the acquisition action in their news feeds. For example, a customer can sign a petition, support projects, or demand challenges in their news feeds. When they click the action in their update, they're directed to a single page where they complete the action.

This isn't meant to replace the custom tabs, but it's best used as a powerful addition to your custom tabs.

Boost New Product Announcements

Boost posts on Facebook are still very effective, especially for the smaller businesses. Even though most experts will advise not to use the feature, small businesses can greatly benefit from boost posts announcing new products.

Just because many who are teaching social media tell you not to boost posts, that doesn't mean they don't work or are not effective. Question everything, and test the tactics and techniques for yourself.

Website Custom Audiences

Facebook is moving into what's known as a pay-to-play model, so marketers are going to need to find better ways they can reach their fans. While you can ads targeting specific fans, one of the best tips for marketing on Facebook is to use Website Custom Audiences instead.

When you use Website Custom Audiences, you can run Facebook ads through the Power Editor. This allows you to target those who have visited your website or a certain page on your website when they are back on Facebook.

This is useful for many different reasons.

Let's say someone is reading a guide on your website. If you're running Website Custom Audiences, when they go back over to Facebook, instead of seeing their normal page posts, they will see a template to download pertaining to your guide.

If someone is reading an article about how to use one of your products, they can be targeted on Facebook with a link to a video on how to use that product on their Facebook news feed.

While these are just a few ways you can use this tool to improve your marketing on Facebook, there are numerous others out there. The key takeaway is to get creative with how you target your audience. You can generate more leads and better customers with your Facebook marketing efforts if you move beyond the norm.

Increase PR Efforts

With everything that Facebook offers for their marketers, it's easy to lose sight of the fact that it is a tool that supports your brand's PR efforts. The truth is that reporters rely on Facebook so as to source stories and Facebook endorses the platform as a Rolodex with a billion contacts for the reporters.

Where your company might have relied on a press release previously, now you can share your story on Facebook. It' provides a low-friction option for reporting the facts in the case of breaking news or providing comments on emerging issues that are going to help you get your story to the media and the public quicker.

You can research members of the media using Facebook Graph Search. This tool allows you to quickly figure out who works where, what websites and publications your fans might read, or follow those who have a journalism-orelated public title. When you search for a journalist and the name of the media outlet, you can find potential contacts.

In addition, actively monitoring Facebook pages of your target media can be a good way to position your company or brand as a source for stories. Many media channels will petition sources through their social media accounts. You can make a notice list of your chief pages in one spot to observe them on a continuous basis.

Split Testing Facebook Ads

Facebook advertising has become critical for marketing efforts of companies, and using it effectively without wasting money means you have to find the perfect keywords.

The way you can do this is to split test audiences. Split testing is taking a percentage of the advertising budget and running ads while changing only a single item at a time and comparing the results to see which ad performed better.

The structure of the Facebook ad campaigns has changed a little, and you can turn on and off the ads automatically at the Ad Set level. Structure your campaigns to run one ad below every ad set so that you can easily turn them on and off at their set times.

Many people want to know how large their target audience should be, but this will depend on many factors, so there isn't one right answer to this question. There are many people who benefit from targeting narrow audiences, while others do better targeting wider audiences. Split testing will be the only way to determine the answer for your brand.

Determine how well the ad performs by looking at the one that gets the cheapest clicks for whatever the goal of your ad is. If your ad is driving people to your website, the best ad is going to receive the cheapest website clicks. If you're able, make a conversion pixel to observe which ad converts best on the website.

Split testing doesn't have to be expensive or hard, and it's going to save you a lot of money in the future. If you can test five to ten different audiences at twenty-five to fifty dollars for each ad, then you'll have two to three perfect target audiences for future ads.

Running Facebook Promotions and Contests

For years, Facebook has said that promotions and contests had to be run through applications and not on timelines, or walls, as people used to call them. Companies were not allowed to ask someone to comment or like a picture or a post to be entered to win. However, that's all changed.

Facebook announced they'd changed their terms to make it easier for businesses to make and run promotions on Facebook. They're letting pages run contests and promotions on their timelines. According to Facebook, businesses can now collect entries by having someone comment, like, or post on a page or a post. They can collect entries by having the users message the page, and they can utilize the likes as a voting mechanism.

Businesses with Facebook pages have many more options now, and they can run a contest quickly by posting a photo or text and asking people to like or comment on that post. You can get a lot more engagement on your page by running contests.

Rules for Promotions and Contests

1. If you're using Facebook to administer a promotion or communicate, you are responsible for the lawful operation of the promotion, including the official rules, the eligibility requirements and offer terms, compliance with regulations and rules governing the promotion and prizes offered.

2. Promotions on Facebook have to have a complete release of Facebook by each participant or entrant, and an acknowledgment that the promotion is no way endorsed, sponsored, or administered by Facebook – or even associated with Facebook.

3. Promotions have to be administered in apps on Facebook or on Pages on Facebook. Personal timelines cannot be used to administer a promotion – 'share your timeline to enter' or 'share your friend's timeline to get entries.'

4. Facebook will not assist in the administration of the promotion, and the business agrees that

if it uses the services to administer the promotion, it does so at its own risk.

Do's and Don'ts of Facebook Contests

1. **Do** require that people post a comment or like a post to be entered in the contest.
2. **Do** require someone post something directly on the company's timeline to enter.
3. **Do** use likes as a way to vote.
4. **Do** require someone message the page to enter.
5. **Do** announce the winner on the business' page.
6. **Do** require entrants to have to come back to the page to see who has won the contest to win the prize.
7. **Do** use the like button plugin on a website as a way to vote.
8. **Do** use an app plugin to post entries to the contest directly to the page.
9. **Do** run the contest through the Facebook app.
10. **Don't** require that someone share a photo or post to be entered.

11. **Don't** require that someone post something on their timeline or a friends' timeline to enter the contest.
12. **Don't** require someone to tag themselves in an image to vote or enter.
13. **Don't** have anyone who likes the page be entered to win.

If you're wondering if the contest is going to work within Facebook's rules, think about where the engagement is going to happen. If it's directly on the page's timeline or through the message app, then it's probably alright. You can still use third-party apps to run contests.

In addition, take note that you can encourage people to share the contest or post, but you can't require them to do so for entry. Many third-party apps use to require people to share the page to get extra entries, but that practice is will soon come to an end.

Choosing What Type of Contest to Run

With more options comes the hard decision of what type of contest to run. You can break it down into these two options.

- Facebook timeline contests that give you more engagement quickly.
- Facebook app contests that give you a list of email addresses you can keep.

However, there are a few more consideration than these basic needs. You should take into account the pros and cons of each type of contest before you decide.

Timeline Contests

- **Pro** – easy and quick to setup.
- **Pro** – easy and fun to engage with participants.
- **Pro** – free to run
- **Pro** – works on mobile devices
- **Pro** – an increased PTAT score
- **Con** – you don't receive email addresses with the entries.
- **Con** – you are unable to re-share posts easily to tell people about the contest more than once.
- **Con** – you have to post the rules of the contest and a release of Facebook's

responsibility for the contest somewhere in the post.

- **Con** – it most likely won't increase fans as much as the app would.
- **Con** – it could be harder to notify winners if they're not paying attention.
- **Con** – if you require a comment and a like to enter, it could be difficult to validate.

Facebook App Contests

- **Pro** – you can gather email addresses to connect with potential clients or customers again.
- **Pro** – there's more control over how the contest looks and feels.
- **Pro** – you can make like-gated entries so you can grow your fan base.
- **Pro** – you can easily re-share to promote the contest multiple times.
- **Pro** – the rules can be posted in the app easily.
- **Pro** – there are numerous contest apps that have measurements to show data about when people have entered and where they've entered from.

- **Con** – the barrier to entry is a bit higher.
- **Con** – some contest apps don't work on the mobile devices.
- **Con** – there's a cost to this type of contest.

Best Practices for Contests

Timeline contests are excellent for businesses to utilize. However, there are some best practices you should follow on your Facebook contest.

1. **Use a picture to describe the basics of the contest.** Pictures are shareable and more engaging than text posts, and the text travels with the picture while it's being shared.

2. **Required comments.** If you require someone to comment, you can tag the person who's won in a comment when you've selected the winner.

3. **Make the rules clear in your post.** Give the participant basic, clear rules for them to follow. If you need more space, you might want to host the rules on your website and refer people there using a link.

4. **Pin your post on the top of your page for visibility.**

5. **Make the length fairly short.** It's hard to re-post the link, so make the length of your contest no more than a week.

6. **Use apps for bigger prizes or for when you'd like to collect leads and emails.** Apps are easier for you to promote, and you can connect some of them directly to your email provider to easily synchronize the emails you collect.

Overall, Facebook is one of the giants of the advertising world when it comes to social media marketing, and, they're a great place to start. There are over a billion people you can impress on facebook, as well as relatively inexpensive options for advertising your company's page, posts, and contests. However, if Facebook isn't where you'd like to start, then Twitter might be your next best bet.

Chapter Three – The Secret Tips to Marketing on Twitter

There are 974 million users on Twitter; however, only 241 million people log on once a month. Compared to Facebook's statistics, it might seem like Twitter wouldn't be the best place to start. However, statistics reported by CNN suggests a majority of the people who are logging onto Twitter are seeking information and not entertainment, which means businesses can easily attract the attention of potential customers or clients looking for more information.

Using Twitter for Business

When it comes to marketing on Twitter, your bio and your audience are very important. We're going to take a look at how you can optimize your Twitter results by following a few simple steps.

Optimize Your Bio

You want to make sure your company identity and voice are all branded well. This means having a bio that tells your audience who you are and includes a link to the company's webpage or their landing page. Have a consistent tone between the Twitter account and the landing page, so your audience has a clear understanding of who you are and what you do.

Find Out Influencers and Experts in the Target Areas and Interact With Them Regularly

Use Twitter search or tools such as Topsy to figure out where like-minded prospects, influencers, and customers are by searching for keywords that relate to your industry. Then follow them and interact with them on a daily basis.

You should make a list of the top one hundred most prominent businesses and people in your niche – thought leaders, journalists, potential customers, writers and bloggers, potential partners, etc. Then, add them to your private Twitter list and participate with them on a day-to-day basis. Tools such as Hootsuite will make it easier to manage this process. Remember to be helpful and casual rather than promotional. Build a relationship with these people and look for opportunities where you can collaborate together.

Get Your Colleagues Involved

The first people who are going to help you build your brand are going to come from inside the company. Make sure co-workers are following on Twitter and engaging with posts by tweeting, retweeting, and commenting.

Tweet Regularly

Tweeting on a regular basis is a sign of a healthy, active profile. If you only tweet once a week, or even once a month, you're not going to keep up with people on Twitter, or even worse, people are going to forget about you.

Daily tweets and engagements are a great way to stay in front of your customers. Just be sure you tweet relevant information that's useful to them. That way, they retweet, comment, or favorite your posts.

Ask for Twitter Love

Ask your followers to retweet, mention, or favorite tweets, or share content with fresh tweets. People like to know they're helping their favorite brands, so don't be afraid to ask them for a bit of help getting the word out there.

Track Mentions and Respond

You need to track keywords and brand mentions in order to be sure you know what's being said. Be sure you respond in a professional, polite manner if it's appropriate to respond at all. Customer service is the best marketing tool you have, and many customers will post their complaints and product questions on Twitter. You want to be there to show you can help.

Setup your Twitter searches for terms that are relevant to your business. Monitor the conversations in these searches and jump in when it's appropriate. For example, if you're a dentist, you can set up a search term for dentist on Twitter in your area, say Philadelphia, so the search term would be 'dentist Philadelphia.' Then, when you see that someone has tweeted they need to go to the dentist, but it's difficult to get an appointment, you can jump in and let them know you have spots open for new patients.

Retweet

You shouldn't be afraid to retweet because this helps you link with and cement your thought leadership in the industry you're in. Plus, people love it when their tweets are retweeted by businesses!

Favorite Tweets

There are many people who don't know how favoriting tweets works, but it gets someone's attention more than a retweet or a mention.

Follow Hashtags or Trends

You should take a look at trending hashtags and topics and figure out a way to make a relevant connection to your brand. By putting your business in the trending topics, your handle is going to be seen when people search for tweets regarding that specific topic.

Tagging posts with a few trending and relevant hashtags will help you reach new users. However, hashtags need to be used sparingly because people see them as Twitter spam when they're overused or attached to content that's not relevant.

Offer Special Deals and Discounts

Run some Twitter contests, such as, the next fifty people who retweet this post will receive a coupon for fifty percent off or have them post pictures of themselves using the product or in the store and have a random drawing.

Use Images and Videos

Get visual by using videos and photos. They obtain three to four more times the amount of clicks on Twitter than text posts.

Images and videos have proven to receive more clicks, view, and shares than a plain text tweeter. While a community manager might be doing a good job engaging followers, a post about enjoying the weekend is much less effective than in-stream content where someone can view a film trailer and figure out where the movie is playing in their neighborhood. In fact, research has demonstrated that rich tweets have a lot less negative feedback ratings because customers appreciate content that's easier to see on their mobile devices.

Promote Tweets

You want to invest in promoted tweets because it directly targets your audience. Failing to define who you're trying to reach can cost you a lot of time and money. Be sure your promoted tweets aren't spammy, though. The goal is to provide value that establishes credibility and trust with your followers, not trick people into clicking on a link.

Keep it fresh. Be sure your promoted tweets are not running for too long. If you'd like to continue to get that message across to your followers, then find a different, new way to say it.

Make Twitter integrated with other marketing efforts

Like other social media platforms, Twitter is a lot more effective when it's integrated with other marketing activities. For example, if you run a promotion or contest on Twitter, allow your email subscribers to know about it because they are another customer base who have already let you know they want to receive messages from you. When you occasionally tweet out a link to your mailing list, you can connect your Twitter base with your email list.

Use Twitter Analytics

Just as you should use Facebook's built-in analytics, you should be using their native analytics to get a grasp on what's working and what's not with your audience. In the analytics dashboard, you can tell what your best days to tweet are, the type of content that is favorited, and the demographics of the followers your brand is attracting. You can then replicate what's working and reevaluate what's not.

Twitter Marketing Plan

Twitter is a bit different from other social media platforms, so we're going to go over a quick plan before you begin building your audience.

#1: Set Objectives

It's imperative you decide what you'd like to achieve before you plan your strategy for Twitter. If you'd like to get more people to view business content, your objective should include:

- Generate leads by obtaining views from followers on the landing page.
- Create awareness for a new service or product by using Twitter to market it to relevant potential customers or clients.
- Build a positive image of the brand, services, and products by using tools like Twitter's PR tool.
- Build a community of people who are like-minded to give you ideas on how to innovate a service, product, or marketing strategy.

- Provide customer support by providing valuable content, and one-on-one conversations that help clients and customers get the most out of services and products.
- Engage in conversations with industry influencers and build leadership by sharing opinions.

#2: Figure Out Where Twitters Fit into the Content Strategy

Your Twitter plan is going to have its own unique identity in your marketing strategy. For example, some things your Twitter strategy can drive in your larger plan are:

- Traffic – you can use Twitter to drive traffic to a company website or blog, and use direct links to posts and landing pages.
- Conversions – you can use Twitter to integrate messages where you're looking for a certain action, such as a subscription sign-up or enrollment.
- Sales – you can use Twitter to increase sales using images, videos, and blog posts.

#3: Identify Target Audiences on Twitter

Before you build an audience, you need to know what your target audience is. There are so many ways to figure this out. You can build Twitter lists for every segment of your audience to keep track of specific demographics that like certain types of content. Here's how you can build targeted lists:

- Search for keywords in their bios – use tools such as Followerwonk or SocialBro to search for users with keywords in their bios. You can search by location, too.

- Look at hashtags – use trade related hashtags and look through streams to figure out who's viewing them. Brainstorming sessions will help you find the best hashtags for marketing goals.

- Engage and follow – use Twitter tools such as Tweetdeck and Hootsuite to import Twitter lists into columns. This makes it easier to follow lists and build relationships with those in the list.

#4: Determine Best Times to Tweet

Not everyone is going to be on Twitter twenty-four hours a day, seven days a week. You have to figure out when most of your followers are online, and that's when you should tweet.

Some things you ought to consider are where you're located, and whether your followers are on during the day or night.

Here's how to figure out the best times to tweet for the most interaction:

- SocialBro – analyzes the timelines of those following your business account and generates reports that show you when you ought to tweet to reach them.
- Hootsuite Autoschedule – if you are using Hootsuite, this feature already knows the times of day your tweets get the most engagement.
- Tweriod – this runs an analysis of followers and shows when they're online, as well as the best times to tweet to reach them.

#5 Getting Content Ideas

For most content marketers, Twitter is the favorite destination to get great topic ideas. If you need to brainstorm on the next blog post or eBook topic, try these strategies.

- Enter keywords – enter the relevant keywords for your business and check out what's being mentioned. There might be many different articles, discussions, announcements, and more that's happening right in front of you. These are going to show you what's popular, what your target audience desires, and what influencers are talking about.

- Follow the network – followers are tweeting about the industry you're in, and they can give you some great ideas. For example, if you see that people are asking a lot of questions about a specific strategy, you could write tutorials about it.

- Look out for pain points – your potential clients and customers have questions and issues. They might be attempting to engage on Twitter to obtain a solution. Keep an eye on what's happening to know what questions you should answer.

#6: Monitor Competitor's Tweets

Twitter is a very popular network for brands, which makes it easier to see what the competition is doing. Monitor their accounts to see what's getting them the most engagement from clients.

- Follow competitors – you don't have to follow them, technically. Make a private list that's only visible to you. Add the competitors, and you can include employees of competitors if there is more than one primary account.
- Monitor engagements – know what people are saying about them, as well as how they respond.
- Look at articles they share – if they are creating a ton of content, this is going to help you see how they're marketing their content, as well as how their audience receives it.

#7 Choose What You Share

You ought to share a variety of content on Twitter, not just text posts. The network will support a lot of different formats for media that can be embedded into tweets, such as:

- Text – this sweet, short, and simple tweet form is good for news, updates, asking questions, and quick facts.

- Photos – this is a good way to enhance your message. Photos will stand out more, and get more impressions and more engagements on your content.

- Videos – if a picture is worth a thousand words, then a video will speak millions. Videos integrated into messages work wonders to put messages in front of the proper audience. Embed a short and informative video for your followers.

- Slideshare – these are a boon for visual information but don't keep your presentations to one platform. With a slide deck, you can present a lot of content in easy to digest ways.

- Links – if there's a valuable piece of content pertaining to your business that is on your site or somewhere else, then embed a link or just post it on your feed. Add a hashtag to boost reach and give a clear idea of what the link will lead to.

#8: Promote Content

If you use Twitter well, you can drive a lot of traffic to your website. However, just tweeting the title of your blog post with a link back to the website each time will not work. You have to be creative when you craft tweets to promote blog videos, posts, and content. Here are a few ways to get more clicks.

- Make it short – tweets that are a hundred or fewer characters often get higher conversions. When promoting a link, write a brief introduction; it should be just enough that the reader knows what they should expect when they click on the link.
- Quote posts – try using teasers from your posts. The quote should be precise and give the reader a good idea of what the post will be about.
- Include statistics – people love figures and facts, so use stats that support your arguments in your content. This will add validity to ideas.

- Leverage the hashtags – these are an excellent way to reach members of the industry who don't follow you as of yet. Use the common industry ones to do this. You can use branded hashtags and encourage other people to use them, too.

- Use the @mentions – if your post mentions a publication or an industry influencer, make sure you mention them in the promotions. They're going to be flattered, and there is a good chance they're going to share it too, so, you'll reach an entirely new audience.

- Ask for shares – this is an excellent way to get tweets retweeted. Just ask the viewers to retweet the post. Tweets that specifically ask for retweets are highly likely to get them.

- Promote tweets – if you want even more exposure than what you're already getting, promote your tweets for a small investment. They're easy to make and will bring you a lot of traffic.

Building an Audience

Building and maintaining your audience can seem time-consuming even to those familiar with marketing, whether it's from scratch or from an established audience elsewhere. Posting a few times a day is not enough to encourage growth. This is why it's important that you actively try to grow your Twitter audience on a daily basis. To see the real growth in as little time as possible, you have to understand and be direct with your goals.

If you set and implement this routine, in as little as half an hour a day, you can begin to see more significant and quicker growth in your audience.

The Strategy Overall

The idea behind this active audience growth is that you will go out there on Twitter and discover the users that are interested in your industry and niche, and target the ones who are in the middle of conversations about your topic and industry. Then you will insert yourself into the middle of this conversation in a non-spam way that adds value to their conversation.

For example, if you have an account for your online store that's selling guitars, you could search for Twitter users who are discussing guitars or inquiring about how to play them, and then engage with them.

Don't pitch to them, ask them to check your website, or ask them to follow you. Just help them.

More often than not, they're going to check you out to see who you are, see your bio, and click on your link to your website. They may even follow you.

There's a little bit more to it than this, including following and favoriting the relevant users, but overall, engage with those who could be interested in your products or services and add some value to their conversations. This could seem a little more underdog than you're used to, but it works.

Optimize that Bio

After you've first interacted with someone, they're likely to click on your profile to learn more about who you are. First impressions are everything, so you need to make sure your Twitter bio and profile are optimized for that good first impression.

The first thing you need to have is a profile picture that's easily identifiable so that when you appear in their notification feed after you've followed them, favorited them, or replied to a tweet, it's immediately clear who you are and what you're about.

Brands should forgo logos for more memorable and relevant images. For example, if you're a guitar store, then use a picture of a guitar.

The following thing you should consider is your Twitter handle or name. If you're interested in getting a guitar player on Twitter to look at your profile when they see you in the notifications, you need a name that's identifiable for them. For example, if your store's name is Rad, then a better name on Twitter could be Rad Guitar rather than Rad because guitar players will see Guitar in the name and they will want to learn more about you.

Finally, you should use pinned Tweets to assist in inspiring people to follow you. Once they've clicked to view your profile once you've shown up in their notifications, what do you want to let them know? Why should they be following you rather than someone else? What do you tweet about all the time? Your pinned Tweet lets you talk about yourself in a bit more detail than your bio does. It can be used to send profile visitors to landing pages where emails can be collected, too.

Discover and Engage with Twitter Users

You should be using the search link **search.twitter.com** to find those who are having conversations about your niche or industry, but what should you search for and how should you be searching?

The first thing you need to consider is using an operator to filter out excess results. You need to find those who are truly discussing what you're searching for and are really engaged with your industry or niche. You can use Twitter's Advanced Search, but operators are nicer because they let you filter out and choose more selections, such as sifting out Tweets that have links. Here are a few you can try out.

- -filter:links – this is going to let you filter out Tweets that have links in them. Usually, Tweets that contain links are promotional tweets and not real conversations or questions about the topic.
- " " – if you're looking for a specific phrase, include it in quotes so that results only have Tweets with this phrase in them and not Tweets that have those words. It's worth investigating with searches and including and

excluding quotation marks around the phrases to see what you get.

- ? – if you're looking for users who are asking questions, then this will only show tweets that have questions in them.
- lang:en – this will set the language for the results you're looking for, which in this case, is English.
- Near:"Washington" – find Tweets from users who are located near you or at a specific location you want to search. This is good for if you're a local business.
- -word – if you want to filter out tweets that have specific words or phrases, then use a dash with that word.

Now you know how to cut out some of the noise in your search results, so let's find people who are actually talking about what you care about and engage with those people.

Let's continue to use the guitar store example, and you'd like to build up your following on Twitter. Maybe you want to find people who are talking about bass guitars only. Put in the search terms: **"bass guitar" – filter:links**.

Now, it's as easy as engaging with those who are most excited and passionate about the topic at hand in these results. These are the people you want to engage because you'll get a response from them, and they are going to check your profile and maybe follow you.

Remember, add value to the conversation rather than trying to pitch or sell random people on your business.

Grow by Following Users

Another part of organically and actively growing a Twitter following is to follow the users who might be interested in your business or brand. Look at the users who are 'followers' of competitors or influencers in the niche your business is in.

From there, follow the people you believe might be interested in your business. This is a proven way to grow a following, but there are a few things you should keep in mind while doing this.

You shouldn't overdo it. Follow about fifty people a day, and be sure they're highly targeted followers. Follow people who are active, and don't follow other businesses.

You should maintain a good ratio of following to followers. One to one is alright when you're beginning; otherwise, you'll come off as being a spammer. Use TwitNerd weekly to see who hasn't followed you back after a few days.

It's important to unfollow people who are not following you back within a few days so that you maintain the proper ratio. You need to be careful with the number of unfollows you have in a day. Twenty to fifty per day is a safe range, and you don't want to exceed this; otherwise, Twitter might flag you as someone who is abusing the system.

Twitter might not have as many people who are active on it as Facebook, but the people who are active are serious about obtaining information, which makes it easier to interact with them. It's much easier to find your audience on Twitter than it is on Facebook, which is why many companies choose to begin with Twitter.

Chapter Four – How Instagram Isn't Just for Budding Photographers

Instagram is a great tool to use, but you have to know how to use it. Most businesses like to engage users who post photographs for them, but you can easily post your own for your business and obtain even more followers. So why choose Instagram over the other social media websites out there?

Well, Instagram has over half a million active users every month. These users have shared over forty billion photos since the conception of Instagram, and they share an average of ninety-five million photos and videos every day. Eighty percent of the users come from outside of the United States, and it's used by 24% of American men and 31% of American women. Therefore, if your business is focused more on an international level, then Instagram might be a good answer for you. Plus, it can mean a lot of exposure if your photo or video goes viral.

So how do you use Instagram? In this chapter, we're going to go over twenty-five ways your business can use Instagram to boost customer interaction and sales.

#1: Get Familiar with Instagram using a Business' Perspective

Businesses have been signing up for Instagram immensely lately. In response, Instagram began a blog for businesses to follow that offers brand spotlights, tips, news, and API examples for businesses to use. Their blog is definitely going to keep you updated on how they operate, so it's a good idea to begin reading that on a regular basis immediately.

Check out their blog and keep up with some of the more unique ways to use Instagram for your business.

#2 Balance Fun Images with Images from Your Business

You should take advantage of the increased real estate your business has with the Instagram page by telling a story with the images you post. Make sure there is a good balance between fun images and the images that reflect your business.

Puppy pictures can receive thousands of likes and pictures of personal shoppers posing at luncheon events will receive half that amount of likes. You should be keeping track of the engagement your images get to figure out what your followers prefer.

#3: Build a Following

There are three main ways you can obtain a following in Instagram. If you already have a Facebook account, then connect the two. If not, then use some popular, relevant hashtags connected to your images. Or you can engage by liking others and following their photos.

Cross-post selected images to the business Facebook page with hashtags that align with your brand image to help potential customers find you on Instagram.

#4: Debut Videos

The recent additions of Instagram's Video on Instagram have given Vine, a Twitter video feed, a serious competitor. There's a filter enabled, fifteen seconds, editable video functionality that's comparable to Vine's 6.5 seconds.

#5: Embed Instagram Videos into Blogs or Websites

Instagram recently released an embed feature for desktop web browsers so that you can embed your videos into your blog or business website. Because you never know who is going to see your shares on a social networking platform, embed the Instagram video to extend the reach of your content.

#6: Follow Followers Back

The people you're following on social networking platforms will make all the different in the world. Many brands on Instagram, some who have a very large following, don't follow their followers back. You should find the brands and people you like and can learn from in your followers, and then follow them back.

#7: Create a Flexible Posting Plan

You don't have to post daily on Instagram; the feed speed on Instagram is pretty laid back. If you begin posting a lot, you could saturate your follower's feeds, and you don't want to force yourself onto their feeds too often. They might unfollow you. Decide what you have ready to post and make a schedule to help you remember what you should be posting when and track what's working once you have a few posts.

#8: Use Apps

There are many apps out there that are going to enhance your photo-sharing experiences. A few you might want to check out are:

- Gramgrab – an app that displays your Instagram photo collection, and allows you to hover over and see the amount of likes, time uploaded, and the filters used for that image.

- Quickagram – lets you browse through some of the random photos listed on your gallery and map. Clicking images will let you open them to their original size, and let you share them on Facebook or comment directly from the page.

- Gramfeed – it's like Quickgram, but it has more features. It's comparable to browsing Instagram using a web browser with links to profiles and the follow button, as well as options for commenting and liking photos.

- Copygram – it's an alternative to Instagram's iPhone app. You can browse photos and users in a grid list view, follow users, comment, and like using the app. There's an option to backup photos by downloading them to a computer, too.

#9: Inspire Your Potential Customers

Post photos that are relevant to not only your brand but also relevant to your potential customers. For example, a whole foods market might post photos that promote healthy, wholesome food items, sustainability, store events, and the active community of employees and customers they have. Attract your target market with images that share an inspiring and compelling story.

#10: Use Filtered and Non-filtered Images

There are numerous filters to choose from on Instagram to change the feel of your images. Some of the most popular filters are:

- Lo-fi
- Velencia
- Rise
- Amaro
- Hudson
- Sierra
- X-Pro II

- Hefe

Filters are more than just aesthetics; they create a theme for your brand. Shake it up every now and again and try filtered and non-filtered images to see what's the most popular with your customers.

#11: Try a Change in Perspective

Rather than constantly pushing your brand or product in an obvious manner, try something new instead. For example:

- Share viewpoints about the world
- Create a unique visual sense
- Train your eye to focus on what makes a provocative, engaging image
- Capture things that are interesting to both your brand and your core customers

#12: Create Photo Contests on Instagram Using Facebook

Now you can host photo contests on Instagram with hashtags to organize the submissions, and RSS feeds to follow along with new photos as they're being added. Use your Facebook status updates to encourage potential clients and customers to enter the Instagram photo contest.

#13: Market Your Brand with Trends

Twitter used to have a #followfriday hashtag that gained a lot of attention. You can use hashtags trending on Instagram to help out your brand. Find some trending ones that pertain to your brand and join in on the fun!

#14: Network

Instagram connects people by using photos, so here are three ways you can create a network:

- Engage by liking and leaving comments on other's photos.
- Follow the established followers from other social media sites.
- Include hashtags if your brand, using specific ones on Google+ and Twitter.

#15: Create an Amazing Profile

Like their counterparts on Facebook and Twitter, Instagram profiles have to include branding information in a specific way. Use the maximum number of characters available to you, pay attention to the wording and tone you use, and use specific image sizes.

Complete your profile with all the information your customers could potentially need to find you and do business with you.

#16 Promote Using both Facebook and Instagram

It's a good thing when a platform such as Facebook purchases another one, which is what happened with Instagram. They are an excellent duo that offers their brands a unique opportunity to promote.

Brands make Instagram videos, share them on their Facebook pages, and boost them into paid media that uses the Facebook news feed in the same way they'd boost a photo or text post. This allows brands to reach the millions of active users on Facebook, which dwarfs the amount of users active only on Instagram.

#17: Qualify and Quantify

If you want to know how your brand is doing on Instagram, there are image analytics tools like Curalate and BlitzMetrics that provide some detailed insights. Curalate can track the likes and comments on posts featured on Instagram, so a brand can see how that popularity translates into how many followers they gain, but it also capitalizes on popularity. Use image analytics to identify the video and images that resonate with followers and fans of your niche.

#18: Reward Your Followers

American Express offers followers on their Instagram profile backstage passes to events such as concerts and fashion shows. Retail brands should reward their followers with promotions and discount codes. Deliver perks to followers, so they make viewing your Instagram feed a priority.

#19: Showcase Employee Photos

Showing employees at work not only gives your potential clients and customers behind-the-scenes access to your company, but it's a great way to celebrate the staff and show them how much you value them. A great way to do this is to share pictures of people who have completed milestones, had successes, or have a special talent.

#20: Treat Followers to Visual Experiences

Find creative ways to showcase the use of your company's services and products. For example, Sharpie demonstrates to their followers how their products can be used to start something creative. Their photos in their feed are of drawings in many different colors using their product.

#21: Use Hashtags Related to Your Industry or Niche

If you're at a location or an event that's designated with a hashtag, then add it to your photos, so attendees and event coordinators are able to find them.

Track the relevance of your hashtags using the Instagram analytics tool Nitrogram, which provides you with metrics such as contributors, engagement, content, and context for hashtags.

#22: Film Important Brand Moments

You can share unique experiences, co-create content with your audience, highlight brand advocates, highlight specific causes, preview products, preview upcoming events by adding visual context, extend your brand's persona, drive promotional awareness, share important news, create videos that show fan appreciation, and leverage your Instagram videos for promotion.

Capture the important moments in your company in a fifteen-second video and share it with your followers, so they feel included in the moment.

#23: Expose Yourself to Other Brands

It's good to follow other brands on Instagram. You can use Statigram to find brands and hashtags that relate to yours by entering the brand name or hashtag into the search box. Search for industry-related keywords and businesses on Statigram, and use it to find, follow, and research competitors.

#24: Expose Something New

News stations will share photos about broadcasts they're going to do later on in the day, and product companies will share pictures of products about to be released. Use Instagram to update your followers when it comes to events, news, or products.

#25: Make it Funny

Yes, running a business is hard work and it requires a lot of dedication, tears, and sometimes some sweat, but it should never be all work without any play. Instagram is a great way to display some fun times in the office or an outing you've had with some coworkers. Sharing these images with your followers suggests that you don't take life so seriously you can't have fun, but it also tells them that you are happy and successful. People like people who are happy and successful.

Add some images that show your human side.

Chapter Five – YouTube for Business

YouTube has statistics very similar to Facebook. They have one billion active users every month, which is about one out of every two people on the internet. People search YouTube for entertainment and educational purposes. This means businesses can easily get in front of their audience with a simple YouTube channel or some videos that demonstrate how to use their products, or what their services can do for their clients.

Using YouTube

So how do you use YouTube? Let's look at a few key points when it comes to posting videos on YouTube before you get started.

Length of Videos

YouTube lets you record videos up to fifteen minutes by default. If you want to make a longer video, you can visit the upload page and click on the 'increase your limit' option. YouTube prompts you to verify your account using a cell phone. Be sure your browser's up to date, so you're able to upload the larger files.

A longer video isn't necessarily better, though. If you're focused on educational content, then it might be hard to fit it all into a few minutes; however, the most viewed videos tend to be less than five minutes. Therefore, don't be afraid to start your experience on YouTube with some small, snappy videos instead of waiting until you have the time to make longer ones.

Video Types

When you're making a video on YouTube, it's imperative you focus on the content your clients, customers, and fans are looking to view. This means your videos have to be oriented toward serving their needs. When was the last time you called your friend and told them to watch the Home Shopping Network? Videos that look like an infomercial are less likely to be shared with others. Providing information and tips people can use for their business or personal use will increase the likelihood of your video being shared. Position yourself as an expert in your niche and use YouTube as your long-term public relations strategy instead of just working on a sale.

Aside from offering tactics and tips, YouTube's a great place to upload some client testimonials. Written testimonials are tricky, and it's hard to determine if the testimonial was made by a real person. Videos, on the other hand, make that person's testimonial much more convincing.

YouTube videos are able to be used to provide office tours, show behind the scenes looks at events, or provide biographies of business leaders and employees. You can interview leaders in the industry you're in, or record a presentation for people who can't attend a meeting.

If you want clients and customers to see presentations you've made without your face in the video, then make screen shares they can see, and then upload those videos to YouTube. You can also broadcast a Google+ hangout or a live webinar directly to a YouTube channel.

Equipment

You can use a flip cam or a webcam to start if you're on a limited budget. Be sure you use bright, natural lighting on your face, record in a quiet room and use headphones to reduce background noises.

Signing Up

To sign up for YouTube, you can sign in with an existing Gmail account if you have one. This integrates well with Google+ and lets you use Google hangouts. You can also sign up with any other existing email address.

When you select your username and your channel name, be sure you use your business name or a specific keyword or phrase pertaining to your industry. You should include the URL for your channel in your marketing materials. Be sure you add a channel description and trailer to help people understand what the channel is about, and what you should expect.

To optimize your profile on YouTube, be sure you include your website URL at the beginning of the video description and the About Us section of your profile. If you put this at the bottom of the description, fewer people are going to see it because they will need to click on the 'more' button to read the rest of the description for the video. In addition, be sure you use the HTTP:// in front of your URL, so it becomes a clickable link. Otherwise, your viewers are going to have to cut and paste the link into their browser.

You'll be able to choose a specific category for your channel when you sign up.

Images and Colors

In the channel settings, under the appearances tab, you can choose your background color and image. A graphic designer is a good person to hire for this to adapt your logo and other images central to your business for the background. Choose a color that matches your company's colors.

In addition to selecting the background image or colors, you should customize your layout in the featured link.

The tabs section will let you determine how the channel is going to show up for others, so be sure to look at the different options and choose the one you'd prefer.

Editing

YouTube has some great editing features to improve videos in the 'edit video' mode. Enhancements will let you improve your video quality using the auto-fix feature, play with lighting, change the style of your video, blur faces, and correct shakiness with the stabilizer feature. You can use the annotations to add links to channels, videos, and playlists, or even prompt viewers to subscribe to the video. In addition, you can add some royalty-free music to your videos, or splice clips from multiple videos in the video editor section.

After Uploading the Video

The video title is a headline for your video, so it should be compelling and descriptive.

Make sure you have keywords in the first two sentences of your description so people searching for that specific information can find it. Google and Bing will search the first few sentences of your description for relevant words. Use tags that describe your video's content, both broad and specific ones. Put the most important ones first, and ask yourself what keywords your viewers might use to find your video.

Make sure you include links to your playlists and channels and inform people how to subscribe.

Featured Videos

Once there are a few videos on your account, you can select one or even a few of them to be featured videos. You can prompt your viewers to view future videos after they've seen certain other videos. Just insert links or titles of those videos in the description.

Sharing Videos

Your videos should be posted on all of your social media platforms if you have others. This helps your content be seen and shared by others. There is a share button below your video that lets you post it on social media's news feed, or you can send a link in your email newsletter.

To upload videos to your website, click the 'share file' button, highlight the code that's provided, and copy that into the HTML editor for your site. You can change the dimensions of your video, so it fits onto your site better.

Don't forget to remind viewers to share the video. As your subscriber list grows, this happens more naturally, but until you have a huge following, ask your key followers to share your video to grow that list.

Privacy Settings

You want to make sure your videos are public, so anyone is able to see them. Yet, you can make videos private if you're still deciding whether you want to use it or not, or if it still needs more editing. If you want to show a video only to those who have links, you can create unlisted videos.

In the tabs area of the profile, you can choose what activity you want to share. For example, you can make comments on other videos private or public.

Reports

YouTube gives you reports you're able to download to figure out how your content is performing. Clicking on the 'analytics' section next to your video manager tab on the homepage of your channel lets you see specific statistics and information on viewers.

It will let you see the top ten watched videos of your channel, as well as playback locations and demographics.

You can see the statistics below the videos by clicking on the 'statistics' link. This will let you see the gender and age of the audience who's viewing your videos, as well as where they're located when they viewed.

Using these analytics, along with other measurements, such as social media shares, the number of people who visit your website directly from videos, as well as direct responses to email newsletters, helps you make better videos over time and can be an important part of a dynamic marketing strategy.

How to Make Videos

With just a bit of an investment and some tools, you can make engaging and fun videos to host on your YouTube channel for your business. Sharing videos via social media, your website, and in your newsletters helps you bring new clients and customers to you, and it helps keep your current ones fans.

Keep the Content Fresh

The most prevalent YouTube networks are the ones that have a high volume of consistently updated content. If you want to use your videos as a marketing tool, then you need to have a lot of videos. There are plenty of ways you can make video content for a small business. Webinars and webcasts can be broken up and posted as series, and you can re-propose your infographics into videos that explain a topic, or you can make short tutorials or product demonstrations. Think about making a corporate company history or profile video. You can interview the staff, customers, or yourself.

Include a Call to Action

You'll most likely have links in the video's description, but you should think about how you'd like your viewers to respond before you post the video. Be sure your calls to action are included in the video. Possible calls to action can include contacting the business for more information, subscribing to the channel, sharing the video on social media sites, leaving feedback, or another desired action you might have.

Get Interactive

As people view the video, they're going to rate the quality and leave comments on it. To keep the momentum going, monitor and respond to feedback as soon as you can. If you can, personalize responses to the visitors, such as answering questions or referring to the comment they left in some way.

Customize the Channel

The YouTube page your visitors view when they click on your name is your channel, and it shouldn't look like every other YouTube page out there. You can customize with colors, links, images, relevant information, and so much more. This is an excellent opportunity to reinforce branding with color palettes, logos, and mottos so that audiences associate this video with your industry or niche.

Put Thought into Titles

People are searching YouTube the same way they search Google – by using phrases and keywords that describe what they're searching for. Titles are heavily weighted on YouTube and in search engines, so don't make it something non-descriptive and boring.

Few people will find a video called 'product demonstration.' Instead, incorporate the content of the video into the title, such as '10 ways to save time with (your company's) app.'

Choose the Right Tags and Category

When you're uploading videos to YouTube, you have to choose a category and enter tags for the video, which are also keywords. There are fifteen categories you can choose from, and you add dozens of tags to your video.

It's good to start with the tags that YouTube suggests for you because they're based on what people are commonly searching for. You can also add some extra tags manually and variations on those tags. For example, if you're selling products for dogs, you can use 'puppy' and 'dogs.'

Write Great Descriptions

The video descriptions on YouTube ought to be informative but short, and they should have many purposes. Describe the video in a sentence or two, and include a link to your business website for those who want to know more.

Consider a Collaboration

Businesses are now starting to collaborate with one another on YouTube. Viewers enjoy collaborative videos because they're an opportunity to see their favorite YouTube channels working with someone else and creators like themselves because they give them additional exposure to a broader audience. Look for some popular YouTube channels that complement your industry or niche, rather than competing, try to pitch an idea of collaboration with them.

Let Customers do the Talking

Small businesses have great results when they post videos of their customer testimonials on their YouTube channel. This is a great way to build credibility and trust with those who might need a little 'nudge' to try a product or service you offer. Video testimonials are proven to have a much greater impact on your audience than a written one.

Use Subtitles

Enabling the subtitles on your YouTube video is pretty simple. Just turn on the auto-captioning and edit the subtitles that come up for accuracy. There are millions of hearing impaired YouTube users who appreciate the captions you add, and they're optional, so they don't bother the viewers who don't like them.

On the other hand, an annotation can annoy a viewer. Resist adding those pop-ups to your videos. Instead, put links to the comments you have in the description.

Don't Confine Videos to YouTube

Just because you're making a YouTube channel, doesn't mean others are going to look for it. As part of your strategy, make sure you spread the word about the channel. When you post new videos, you want to share with others, write blog posts about them, or tweet the link, or perhaps post it on Facebook. You can embed videos on your website, especially product demonstrations and tutorials.

Types of Videos to Make

Just in case you're still wondering what types of videos you can post for your industry or niche, let's look at a few ideas to help you out.

- **Demonstration Videos** – YouTube allows you to show your products in action. This very useful for companies with limited physical distribution channels, including those who tend to sell over the internet rather than in brick and mortar stores. Businesses that use YouTube let customers see their products being used before they make the decision to purchase.

- **Event and Promotion Videos** – YouTube allows you to revisit successful events by displaying the footage of them to those who weren't able to attend, or those who want to share where they were at with their friends. If you run an event, you can share highlights using your YouTube channel. Just make sure everyone in the video has signed a release, or blur their faces.

- **Solve Customer Problems** – Some businesses like to use YouTube to solve their customer's issues with their product. For example, they might post a video on how to install a product, or a screen shot tutorial that shows how to use specific software.

Videos are a great way to address frequently asked questions, troubleshoot issues, or just build your brand. YouTube is a great way to demonstrate to your customers that you're an expert in your field, and they help people understand what your business is all about.

Chapter Six – Social Media Tools Every Business Needs

In this final chapter, we're going to discuss tools every business should consider looking into for their social media marketing efforts. These tools will help you keep track of customers' demographics, make life easier when sharing posts or videos, and streamline your social media experience.

Google Analytics

If you have a blog or *a* website you're hooking your social media account to, then it's likely that Google Analytics is already available to you. If it's not installed, then you should immediately install it on your site or blog.

This program was launched in November of 2005. It's completely free for you to use, and it's much better than a measly visitor counter. Google Analytics allows you to see how many visitors you had that were organic (not repeat), where they are from, how long they were on your site, and what specific pages they were viewing.

It was radically changed in 2011 to include a custom dashboard, real-time statistics, and a powerful social media analytics report that's built in. If you're not tracking the amount of visits to your site, then how are you able to tell if your social media presence is making a difference? Ideally, you want to install this before you start your social media efforts to make sure there's a difference in the amount of visitors when you begin your social media marketing.

Bit.ly

You might think it's odd for a link shortening service to be included in this chapter, but being able to shorten links is a huge advantage. Historically, this was used by social media marketers who were marketing on Twitter because there was a character limit of 140 characters. Using a full URL would be a huge waste of space. Twitter has fixed this issue by creating their own link shortener for their site, so why use this one?

The answer is tracking. Most URL shortening services will not just shorten your links, but they will offer tracking services and analytics for you. When you use the same URL shortener for your social network links, then you can track the social networks from a single dashboard, and see how many clicks you've gotten.

The beauty of this specific shortening service is the analytics. Bit.ly has an amazing amount of information for you. They tell you how many times a link in a tweet was clicked, as well as what network the person was using. If you'd like to be really posh, you can customize the look of your short URL by adding a custom URL shortener. So instead of using bit.ly at the beginning of the URL, it will use yours!

Buffer

Buffer allows you to post or share to all social network platforms you're on. This tool is different from other standard social media management tools because it's mainly for scheduling posts. The advantage is, you can post on Facebook or Twitter when your followers and fans are most likely to be there. Your followers could use Twitter or Facebook in the evening once you're at home relaxing, but Buffer will post automatically at the times you choose during the week.

It lets you post to Facebook and Twitter profiles, pages and groups, LinkedIn profile and pages,

Instagram, and Google+ pages. Whenever you add a post to this service, you choose what network or networks you would like it to go to, and it gets added to the network's queue. When it's time for you to post on your Facebook page next, Buffer posts the first post in the queue and the same for every other network you chose. You don't need to wait for the line, if you want to post immediately, then you can do so.

Sharing your articles is easy to do by using one button in your browser. If you discover an article you know your LinkedIn followers and Twitter followers are going to find interesting, then just click the Buffer button in your browser, add the link and title to those social media networks, and send it immediately or add it to the queue. There are also apps you can use on your mobile devices for Buffer, so you can do this anywhere you have an internet connection!

Do Share

It's a shame Buffer doesn't let you share to your Google+ profiles, but DoShare lets you do it.

With so many social networks out there, how should a small business get the time to invest in all of them?

The only way is by using social media management tools, such as Buffer, which helps you share easily on Facebook, Twitter, and LinkedIn. For Google+, you have to use DoShare. Many social media tools are not integrating with Google+ because Google hasn't released an API for their Google+ profiles.

DoShare lets you post to your Google+ profile and pages through an extension you can use in your browser in Google Chrome. It works in a similar way to Buffer because you can schedule posts throughout the week. The only difference is you need to keep your browser open at the time you would like the post to be posted. If your business has a server or a computer that's on all the time, then this shouldn't be a problem.

Feedly

One of the most imperative lessons for small businesses when it comes to using a social media network is not to make it all about the business. If you're only posting posts about yourself, then you're missing the point of a social network platform. It's about sharing other's content, too. People are more likely to invest in you if you're investing in them, especially if you're sharing content they've posted.

However, how do you find and keep an eye on their content? Build up a list of blogs and websites you want to stay on top of. There are some websites that will produce great content that's interesting and you can share.

Once you have more than five to ten of these, it can be hard to keep up with all of them at once. That's where feed readers come in. Feed reader apps take the RSS feeds from the websites and blogs you'd like to keep an eye on, and lists them for you in an easily accessible way. Feedly is a great app you can use in your browser or on your mobile device. You can save articles for later or instantly share them using Buffer or directly on the social media network you want to share it with. In addition to keeping up with the latest news, this allows you to easily share to all your social media networks during the week.

MailChimp

This is an email newsletter and marketing service that has a proven track record. Every month, MailChimp will send out about four billion emails and take care of all the issues that can come up from sending out emails to customers. Social media is imperative for your business, but sometimes, it takes an email to get them there. You need a valid email address to sign up for likes and comments on Facebook and Twitter, and you have push notifications sent to your phone to alert you when someone has tagged you or updated their Facebook newsfeed. Therefore, email is still important.

Building up a database of email contacts is vital for many small businesses. It allows you to find out more about potential customers and your current ones. MailChimp makes this easy, and over time, you are able to add more information such as demographics, which is helpful for social media marketing strategies.

Making sure your website works well in modern browsers is very challenging. The days are gone where working with Internet Explorer was the only thing you had to worry about. Now, there's Google Chrome, Opera, Firefox, Safari, and a myriad of Internet Explorers to work with. On top of that, there are also mobile apps. MailChimp has spent over ten years making sure email newsletters arrive at customers' inboxes looking as beautiful as they did when you sent them. They have detailed analytics, so you can track recipients when they open your email or click through to a website link.

While many of these features are free, if you want more from MailChimp (wanting to send to more than 2,000 subscribers), then you have to upgrade. However, their prices are reasonable.

LastPass

How many social media sites are you on that require passwords? And how are you supposed to remember all of those passwords when they all require different character limits, upper and lowercase letters, numbers, and symbols? LastPass lets you enter a different password for each social media platform with just one password into their application. It's much easier than you'd expect.

Most people use the same password for every site, but what happens if someone gets a hold of that password? It means they can gain access to every account you have and lock you out of them. Your email account's password is the most important one of all because if a hacker gains access to your email account, they can reset all the passwords of your other accounts.

LastPass works on a mobile device or in your browser. Once you enter the LastPass password, it automatically fills in your username and passwords, so you don't have to remember them. You can use the LastPass Password Challenge to determine the security level of the passwords you enter.

Once you've installed LastPass, take the time to change all your passwords to more secure ones. This app can generate some really complex passwords for you. You'll never need to write down your passwords again!

edocr

Small businesses all have something their customers want, and you have the option of giving away some of that for free. It sounds insane, but it does work. Remember, the golden rule of social media marketing is not to talk about you or your business all the time. If you share content from others, not only will you build relationships with them, but you'll build trust with your customers. Giving away stuff for free is a great way to market, as well as builds trust, too. It shows people you're an expert in your industry. With so many businesses and people out there with social media presences, how can you prove you are who you say you are, and that you're worth speaking to? You give away some of your secrets.

You might have already realized this, and maybe you're doing it with some of your blog posts and your social profiles. However, one of the easier ways to give away stuff is to create an eBook. For example, if you're a bakery, why not make a recipe book for people to download from your site? If you're an accountant, why not make an eBook with tips to keep on top of their accounts? The type of book depends on the type of business you're running, so think about what your customers might want. When people download or read the book, you'll be able to discuss it with them, and maybe some of them will turn into customers.

In order to showcase an eBook on your site, you need to use a document sharing service. You may have heard of services such as SlideShare, which is owned by LinkedIn, but edocr is another good one to use. They're a growing service right now, but when you upload your eBook to their service, you appear in their directory, and you're searchable for any edocr user on the web.

When someone downloads and reads your book, the service will email you to let you know who they are, and you can follow up with them. Another good feature is that you can link the profile to your Google+ profile, which means Google lists your eBooks with you as the author, something that will be more important. Finally, you do have to pay for it, but it's very reasonably priced.

ManageFlitter

Once you begin building followers on Twitter, it can be hard to keep track of the people you follow, as well as those who are following you back. First, use Twitter lists to keep track of them, especially if you're following more than a thousand people. Following a ton of people has a lot of advantages, but it becomes easy to miss some important updates and difficult to interact with those that matter the most. As well as lists, you need a social media relationship management tool.

ManageFlitter is a Twitter follower tool. On the basic level, it lets you see who isn't following you, and then has the option to unfollow a group of these people in bulk. In addition to this, you can find and remove irrelevant or spam followers that are clogging up your

Twitter feeds. One of the best features is the White List, which is a list where you add people you never want to unfollow. These are the people who interact with you on a daily basis and who you want to interact with. All the people on this list are hidden from the ManageFlitter lists so that you can never accidentally unfollow these people.

In addition to this, you can follow people that someone else has followed. This is a great way to follow the same people that are following other businesses in your industry. If they are following a competitor, then they're more likely to follow you.

ManageFlitter has a free plan available, as well as some paid plans. The free plan lets you unfollow up to 200 people a day, in addition to unfollowing fake and inactive accounts. The pro account will let you unfollow as many people as you want per day, as well as follow the followers of other users.

Commun.it
The last recommendation made in this chapter is an app called Commun.it. This app is a social media management tool, but it's a little more specialized

than just that, which is why it's mentioned along with the other social media management tool, Buffer.

This is a social media relationship management tool, which means it helps you discover who's in your community on Twitter. These are the people who support you and the content you tweet – retweeters, favorites, and mentioners – and those who are influencing you.

If you're a small business owner, then you'll have limited time, and Commun.it is a great time saver. Spend just ten to fifteen minutes on this app at the beginning of your work day, and in that time, you can reply to all of your outstanding messages, thank people who have retweeted you, and thank those who are in your community. You can find those who have linked to your blog and engage with them, thank new followers, and interact with those who are on your local lists. In addition to this, you can find out who has unfollowed you and decide whether or not you'd like to unfollow them. Another great feature is interacting with those who are talking about your industry or niche using a monitor engagement list. You can integrate Buffer so that you can schedule your replies.

The core features of this app are free, but pro plans are reasonably priced and allow you to have access to full reporting features, as well as unlimited lead and monitor items, custom groups for up to four Twitter accounts, and engaged members. If you have more than four accounts on Twitter you need to manage, or you need to divide the work between a team, then the business account is most likely for you.

Conclusion

As a final note to this book, we're going to go over some social media etiquette. Most business owners have no idea how to post on social media, and they end up blunder through the process and not getting much reward due to their etiquette. There are some specific do's and don'ts of posting on social media sites, so let's go over some of them in this final section.

Keep Your Target Audience in Mind

The very first rule of social media etiquette is emphasizing the importance of being an interesting conversation partner. Social media channels ought to distribute valuable information that people can share with others, and it should be obtained from a variety of sources. You want to be mindful of what type of content is most engaging for your audience, and what type of content shouldn't be posted. Keep in mind the type of social media account you'd like to follow if it wasn't yours. Deliver the content you talk about in your profile description, and do it at the right times to avoid spamming followers.

Do Not Employ Automatic Messaging

If you're someone who's been on social media before as an individual rather than as a business, then you've most likely received one of these types of messages: "Thanks for following me, now check out my blog/website/podcast." There aren't many people who are interested in a pre-drafted call to action like this.

A few years ago, an individual named Alex Howard, a TechRepublic columnist, tried out an experiment on his social media channels. He sent out pre-drafted messages to about 500 accounts and then asked for people's opinion on what he'd done. While few of them responded positively, most said they treated his message, along with other messages that were similar from other people, as being spam.

His experiment demonstrated that while social media automation comes in handy at certain times, you want to avoid it when you're directly interacting with an audience. This means you should cut back on the automated Twitter comments, private messages on Facebook, and Instagram comments. Rather than attracting new customers to your business, most of these messages will cause the opposite to happen and cost you your current followers. Auto messaging your followers on Twitter can also lead to your brand being labeled as spam and suspended.

The best way you can show appreciation to your followers on social media is to provide them with high-quality content that's shareable, which is what they signed up for when they hit the Like or Follow button. If you'd like to recognize someone individually, then use the **@mention** because it is much more personal and provides them with exposure on your feed they might appreciate.

Respond to Comments Quickly

Communication on a social network is designed to be a two-way street where you get real-time responses to messages, and social media is most effective when it's used this way. Appoint someone to be responsible for looking over social media platforms and monitor for interactions, and make sure they interact with those interactions back. If you get a high volume of interaction on a daily basis, it helps establish an evaluation system to see which ones should be responded to immediately, and which ones are able to wait for a bit.

However, it should be able to go without saying that all comments, especially if they're negative, should be addressed. Ignoring a negative review can lead to the loss of a customer or a really bad public relations disaster. Addressing negative feedback in a timely fashion can help you turn detractors into brand advocates.

Never Badmouth Competition

While you're following the social media accounts of your competitors on social media to get valuable insight on them, you should be careful not to abuse this privilege. Playing with your competitors on social media will go a long way. Not only is it going to help you establish a professional relationship with others in your industry, but it will improve your online reputation in the eyes of your followers, as well as your competitor's followers.

However, that doesn't mean you need to stay silent when another brand calls you out on social media. Take the time to respond to their comment as you would from a customer, especially if the comment is negative. Their audience deserves to hear the other side of the story, yours, in order for them to decide for themselves if the negative messaging from a competitor is worth consideration.

Keep Your Brand Accounts Professional and Separate Personal Accounts

This is one of the most important tips you could follow in this book, and yet it's an important point many beginning social media professionals tend to forget. Keeping the personal account unconnected doesn't just pertain to the apparent protection against unintentionally posting to a work account rather than a personal one. It means you keep the tones of your messages on your branding page in sync, and you make sure all your messages contribute to the mission you've set out for whichever profile you're posting to.

Apart from serving completely different audiences, your personal and business account serve different purposes. This is assuming your business profile takes a neutral position on controversial issues, unless they're a relevant discussion in the industry you're in, and you avoid justification of personal conflicts on your business account.

Don't Spam Followers' Feeds

The best type of conversation is going to be equal parts give and take between you and followers. In social media terms, this means that you keep your social network accounts active without spamming the feeds of your followers. Figure out the best times for engaging with followers on specific channels, and post during those times. Unless there is something urgent, you shouldn't post more than once per hour, maybe even less, depending on the social media channel.

Disperse your messaging across different channels to maintain all your channels consistently and avoid neglecting an account. Social media content calendars are good ways to help you avoid gaps, and pick the best type of content to share with followers.

Never Follow for Numbers

There's a widespread use of follower bots and fake accounts now, so the number of followers you have should not be your primary goal when it comes to measuring the success you have on social media. Avoid indiscriminately following thousands of users in the hopes that they follow you back because this will ruin your feeds with an oversaturation of posts.

The frantic following of random people becomes spam, and it detracts from the value of your follow.

Advertising on social media and creating an influential account on different platforms is imperative for business success nowadays. If you want to increase your sales and get yourself in front of thousands of potential customers, if not millions, then creating a social media profile is important. However, it's better to start with just one and work your way up to having multiple accounts. Once you know how to market on a specific channel, you have to learn how to market on another channel in a different manner.

I do hope the information in this book has helped you figure out the puzzle of marketing on social media. It is my sincere hope that you will utilize the tips in this book to significantly improve your overall marketing skills and make your online business rewarding and of great success.

Thank you for reading!

Made in the USA
San Bernardino, CA
11 March 2017